TREASURY OF
GOLDEN STANDARDS

Produced by
Alfred Music Publishing Co., Inc.
P.O. Box 10003
Van Nuys, CA 91410-0003
alfred.com

Printed in USA.

ISBN-10: 0-7390-7081-9
ISBN-13: 978-0-7390-7081-9

CONTENTS

AIN'T MISBEHAVIN'

Words by
ANDY RAZAF

Music by
THOMAS "FATS" WALLER and HARRY BROOKS

AT LAST

Lyric by
MACK GORDON

Music by
HARRY WARREN

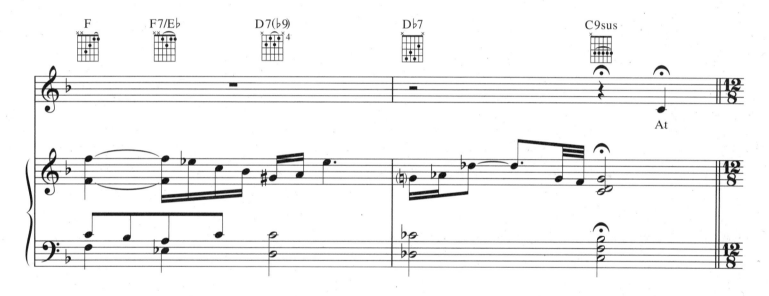

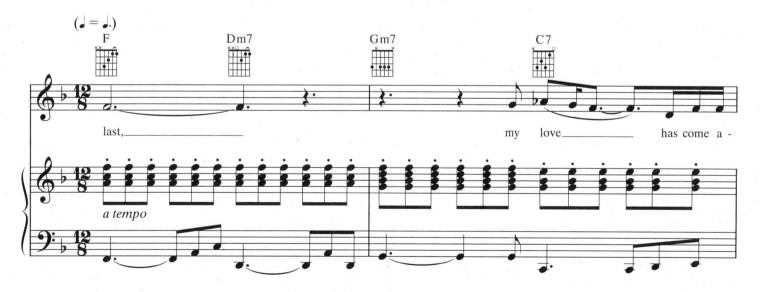

At Last - 5 - 1

was cast,_____ and here____ we are_____ in____

heav - en,_____ for_____ you are

mine,_____ at____ last._____

a tempo (continue 12/8 feel)

AS TIME GOES BY

Words and Music by
HERMAN HUPFELD

As Time Goes By - 4 - 1

AMONG MY SOUVENIRS

Words by
EDGAR LESLIE

Music by
HORATIO NICHOLAS

BEGIN THE BEGUINE

Words and Music by
COLE PORTER

BLUE MOON

Lyrics by
LORENZ HART

Music by
RICHARD RODGERS

Blue Moon - 5 - 1

BLUES IN THE NIGHT

(My Mama Done Tol' Me)

Words by
JOHNNY MERCER

Music by
HAROLD ARLEN

My ma-ma done tol' me____ when I was in {knee - pants,____ / pig - tails,____} my

ma-ma done tol' me,____ {"Son!____ / "Hon!____} A wom-an - 'll sweet talk____ / A man's gon-na sweet talk____} and

Blues in the Night - 6 - 1

BUT NOT FOR ME

Music and Lyrics by
GEORGE GERSHWIN
and IRA GERSHWIN

Old Man Sun-shine, lis-ten, you! Nev-er tell me, "Dreams come true!" Just

try it and I'll start a ri-ot._____

But Not for Me - 4 - 1

Rather slow *(smoothly)*
Refrain:

C'EST MAGNIFIQUE

Words and Music by
COLE PORTER

Moderately

Verse:
freely

Love is such a fan-tas-tic af-fair when it comes to call.

Af-ter tak-ing you up in the air,

down it lets you fall.

But be pa-tient and

C'est Magnifique - 4 - 1

soon you will find   if you fol - low your heart, not your mind,

love is wait - ing there a - gain   to take you up in the

air a - gain.   When

Refrain:
(Slow and easy)

love   comes   in   and   takes   you   for   a

E7

spin, oo la la - la,_____ c'est mag - ni -

Am   **Am6**   **Am**   **E7**   **Am**   **Am7**

fi - que. When ev - 'ry night your

Am   **D9**   **D+**

loved one holds you tight, oo la la - la,_____ c'est mag - ni -

G6   **Gmaj7**   **G6**   **G**

fi - que. But when, one day, your

Verse 2:
When you began of love to speak,
I followed every word,
But when you called love magnifique,
I would have called it absurd.
And when you said it was often tragique,
I would have said it was always comique.
So, mad'moiselle, be sweet to me
And kindly do not repeat to me.

C'est Magnifique - 4 - 4

BODY AND SOUL

Words by EDWARD HEYMAN,
ROBERT SOUR and FRANK EYTON

Music by
JOHN GREEN

Body and Soul - 5 - 1

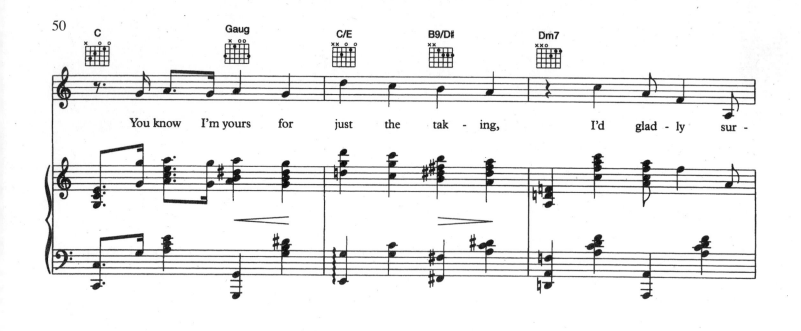

You know I'm yours for just the tak - ing, I'd glad - ly sur -

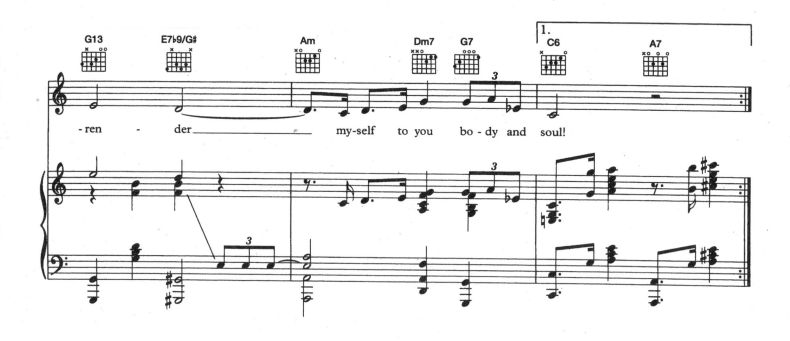

- ren - der _____ my-self to you bo - dy and soul!

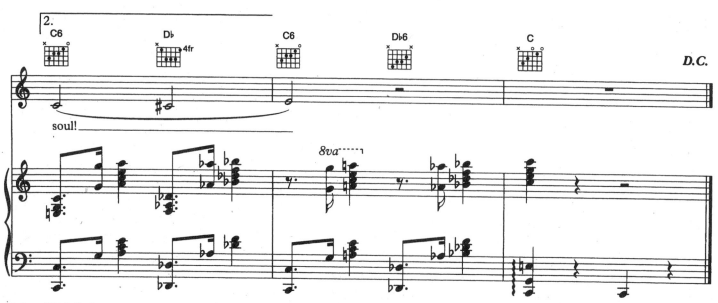

soul! _____

CHANCES ARE

Words by
AL STILLMAN

Music by
ROBERT ALLEN

52

DAYS OF WINE AND ROSES

Lyrics by
JOHNNY MERCER

Music by
HENRY MANCINI

The days of wine and ros - es

laugh and run a - way like a child at play, through the

mead - ow - land to - ward a clos - ing door, a door marked "Nev - er - more," that

DO YOU KNOW WHAT IT MEANS
(To Miss New Orleans)

Lyric by
EDDIE DE LANGE

Music by
LOUIS ALTER

Verse:

I nev-er had this kind-a feel-in'_____

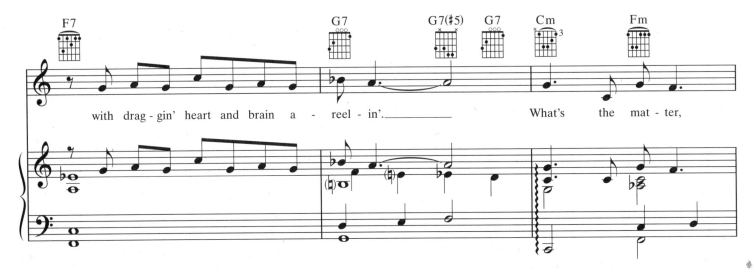

with drag-gin' heart and brain a-reel-in'._____ What's the mat-ter,

Do You Know What It Means (to Miss New Orleans) - 4 - 1

DON'T GET AROUND MUCH ANYMORE

Lyrics by
BOB RUSSELL

Music by
DUKE ELLINGTON

62

club,   got as far as the door.

They'd have asked me a - bout____ you.____ Don't get a - round much an - y -

more._____ Dar - ling, I guess____ my

mind's more at ease.____ But nev - er - the - less,____

DREAM A LITTLE DREAM OF ME

Lyrics by
GUS KAHN

Music by
FABIAN ANDRE and WILBUR SCHWANDT

Dream a Little Dream of Me - 3 - 1

EASY TO LOVE

Words and Music by
COLE PORTER

Billy:

I know too well that I'm___ just wast-ing pre-cious time in think-ing such a thing could be, that you___ could ev-er care for me. I'm sure you hate to hear___ that I a-dore you, dear, but

Easy to Love - 5 - 1

grant me, just the same;___ I'm not en-tire-ly to blame. For...

Easy two (♩ = 60)

You'd be so eas-y to love, so eas-y to i-dol-ize, all

oth-ers a-bove. So sweet to wak-en with;___

so nice to sit down to eggs and ba-con with.___

Oh, how we'd bloom, how we'd thrive, in a cot-tage for two, or e-ven three, four, or five. So, try to see your fu-ture with me, 'cause you'd be oh, so eas-y to love!

EMBRACEABLE YOU

Music and Lyrics by
GEORGE GERSHWIN
and IRA GERSHWIN

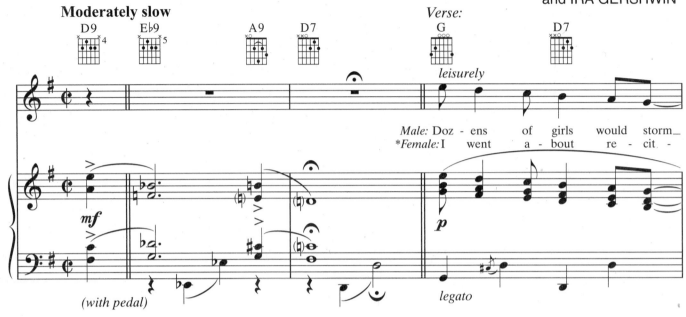

Male: Doz - ens of girls would storm__
Female: I went a - bout re - cit -

___ up, I had to lock my door.
ing, "Here's one who'll nev - er fall!"

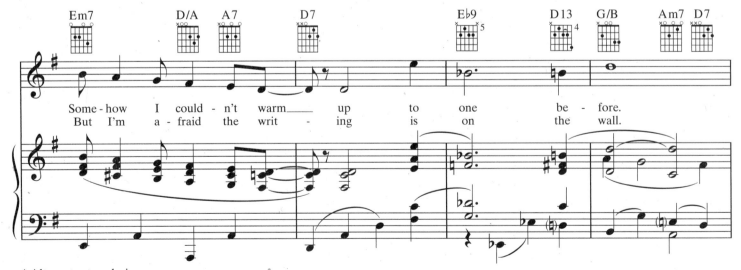

Some - how I could - n't warm__ up to one be - fore.
But I'm a - fraid the writ - ing is on the wall.

* Alternate verse lyric.

Embraceable You - 4 - 1

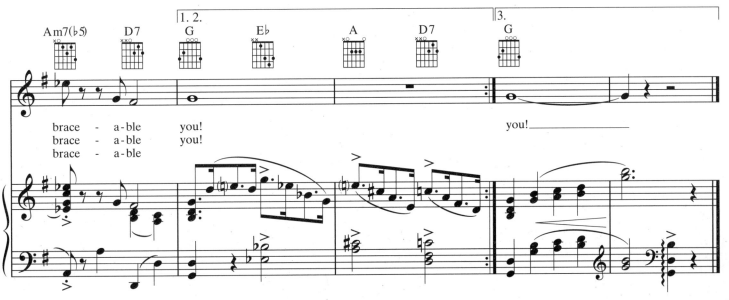

FOOLS RUSH IN
(Where Angels Fear to Tread)

Words by
JOHNNY MERCER

Music by
RUBE BLOOM

Moderately slow (with expression)

Verse:

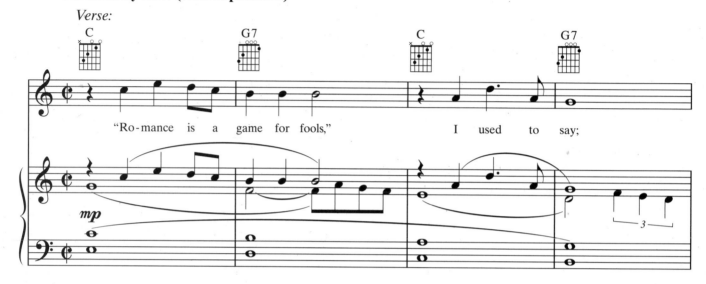

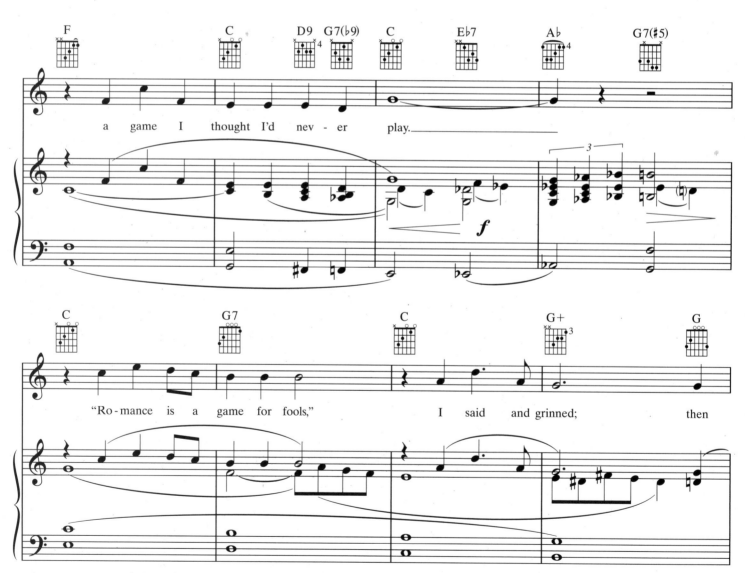

"Ro-mance is a game for fools," I used to say; a game I thought I'd nev - er play. "Ro-mance is a game for fools," I said and grinned; then

Fools Rush In - 4 - 1

Slowly (with expression)
Refrain:

Fools rush in where an-gels fear to tread, and so I come to you, my love, my heart a-bove my head. Though I see the dan-ger

GET ME TO THE CHURCH ON TIME

Lyrics by
ALAN JAY LERNER

Music by
FREDERICK LOEWE

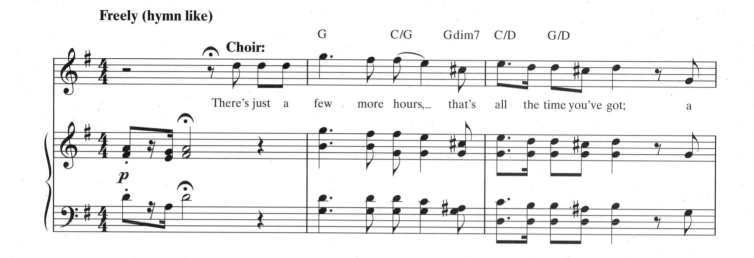

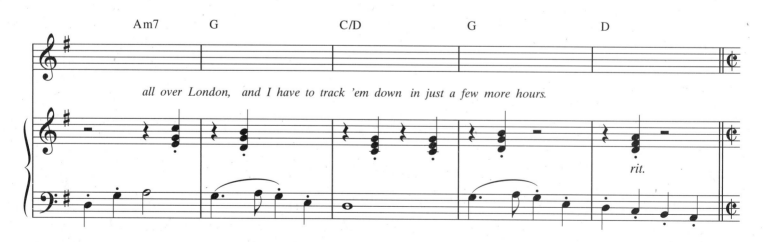

Get Me to the Church on Time - 5 - 1

Good Morning

Words by
ARTHUR FREED

Music by
NACIO HERB BROWN

Good Morning - 3 - 1

HEART

Words and Music by
RICHARD ADLER and JERRY ROSS

HI-LILI, HI-LO

Words by
HELEN DEUTSCH

Music by
BRONISLAW KAPER

A song of love is a sad song; hi-

li-li, hi-li-li, hi-lo. _____ A

song of love is a song of woe; don't

Hi-Lili, Hi-Lo - 3 - 1

HOW ABOUT YOU?

Words by
RALPH FREED

Music by
BURTON LANE

HOW ARE THINGS IN GLOCCA MORRA?

Words by
E.Y. HARBURG

Music by
BURTON LANE

How Are Things in Glocca Morra? - 4 - 1

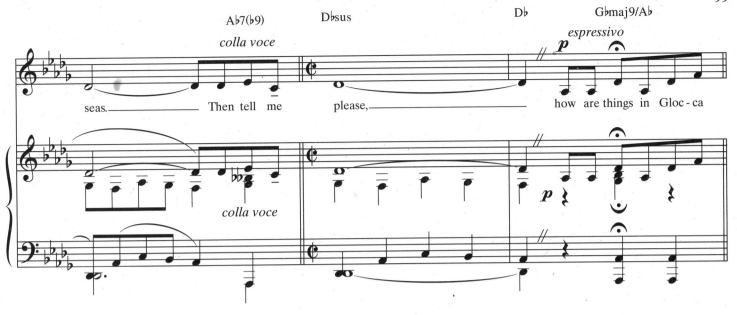

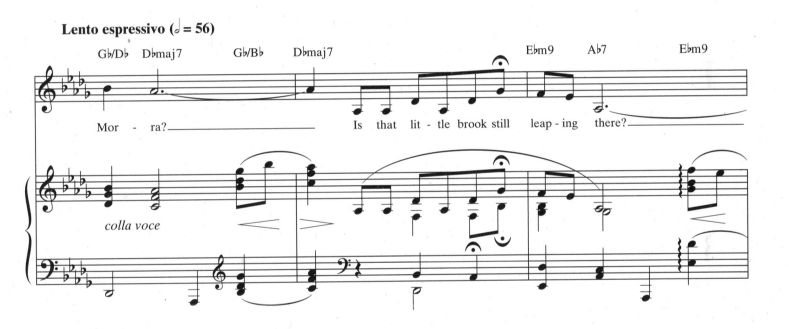

ker - ry and Kil - dare?_____ How are things in Gloc - ca Mor - ra?_____

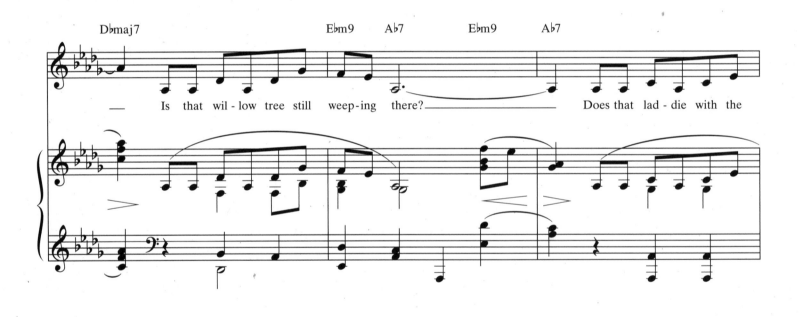

_ Is that wil - low tree still weep - ing there?_____ Does that lad - die with the

twink - lin' eye_____ come whist - lin' by,_____ and does he walk a - way sad and

HOW HIGH THE MOON

Lyrics by
NANCY HAMILTON

Music by
MORGAN LEWIS

Some-where there's mu - sic,_____ how faint the tune!_____ Some-where there's heav - en,_____ how high the moon!_____ There is no

How High the Moon - 3 - 1

I COULD HAVE DANCED ALL NIGHT

Lyrics by
ALAN JAY LERNER

Music by
FREDERICK LOEWE

I Could Have Danced All Night - 9 - 1

But now it's time to sleep.

D.S. 𝄋 al Coda

𝄌 *Coda*

I could have

danced

all night.

I COULD WRITE A BOOK

Words by
LORENZ HART

Music by
RICHARD RODGERS

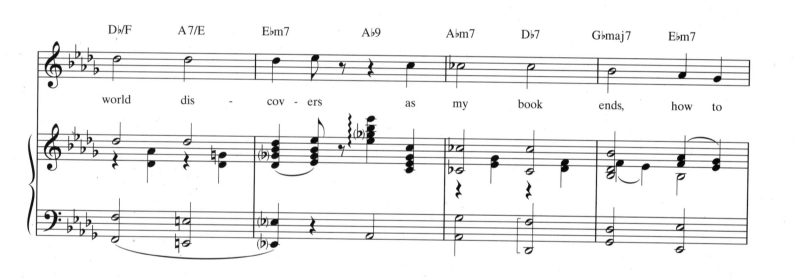

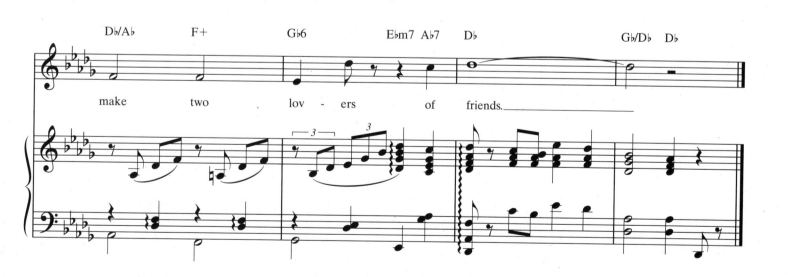

I GOT RHYTHM

Music and Lyrics by
GEORGE GERSHWIN
and IRA GERSHWIN

Refrain:

I DON'T WANT TO SET THE WORLD ON FIRE

Words and Music by
BENNIE BENJAMIN, SOL MARCUS,
EDDIE SEILER and EDDIE DURHAM

I Don't Want to Set the World on Fire - 3 - 1

I ONLY HAVE EYES FOR YOU

Words by
AL DUBIN

Music by
HARRY WARREN

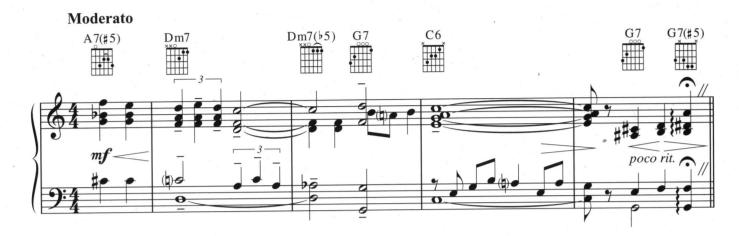

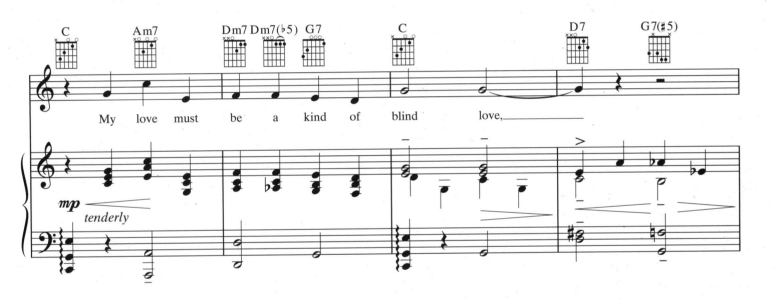

My love must be a kind of blind love,

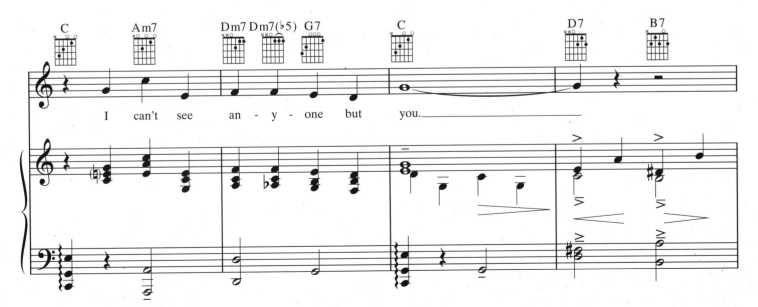

I can't see an-y-one but you.

I Only Have Eyes For You - 5 - 1

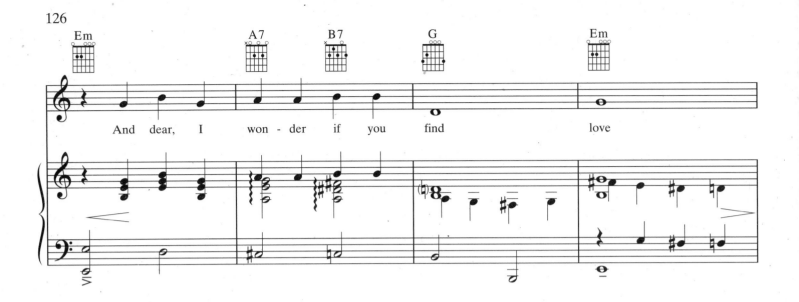

And dear, I won-der if you find love

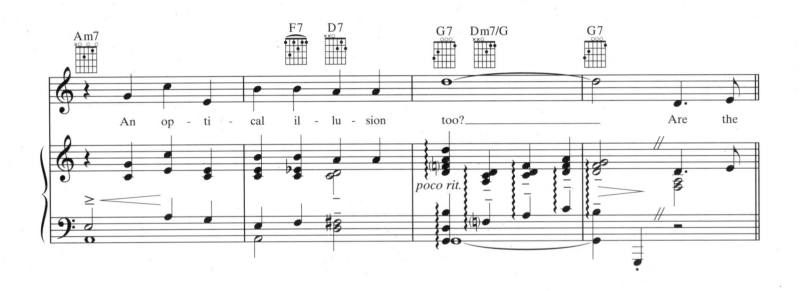

An op-ti-cal il-lu-sion too?_____ Are the

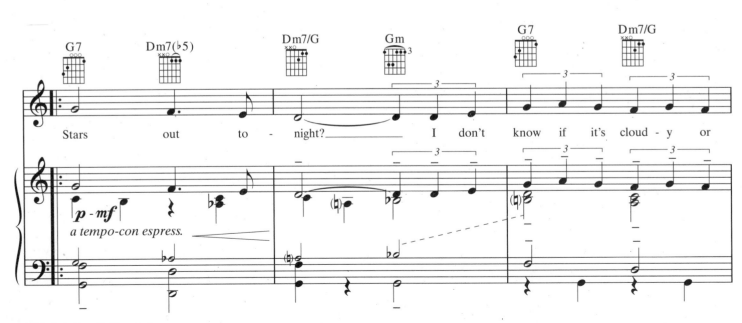

Stars out to -night?_____ I don't know if it's cloud-y or

a tempo-con espress.

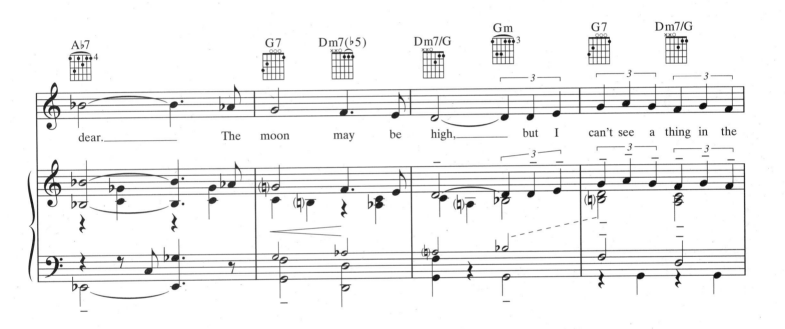

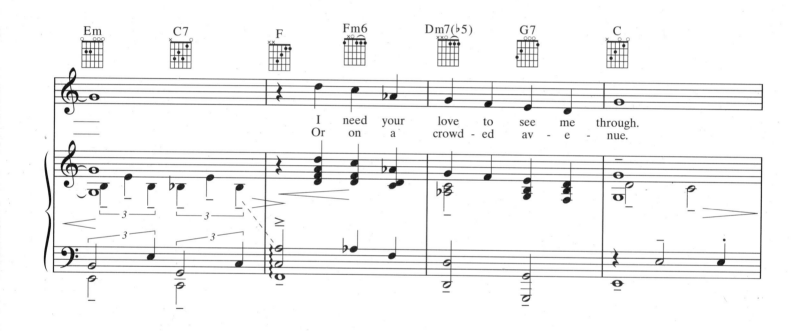

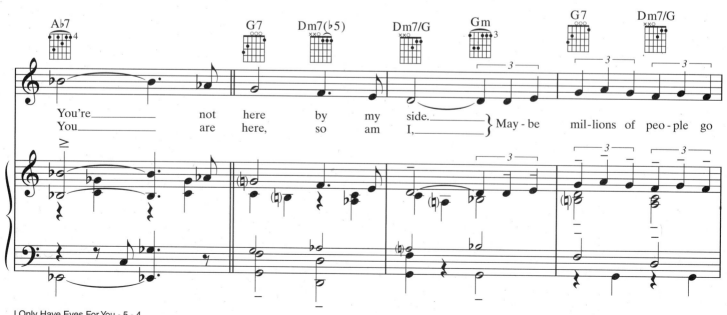

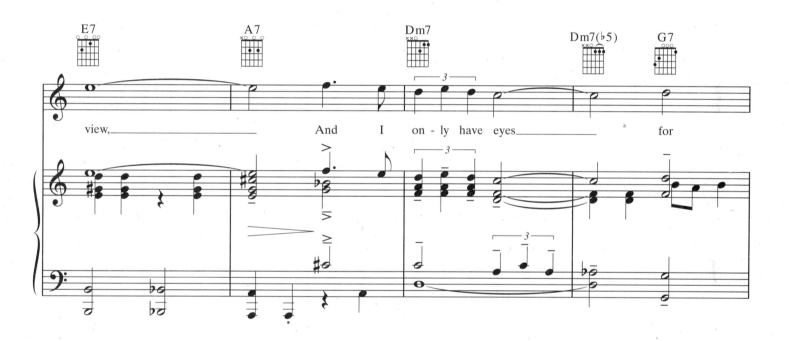

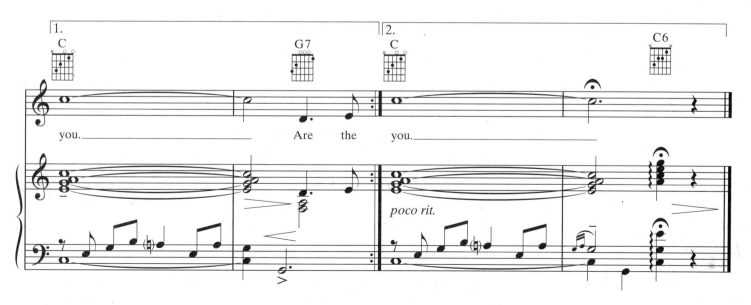

IF EVER I WOULD LEAVE YOU

Lyrics by
ALAN JAY LERNER

Music by
FREDERICK LOEWE

Moderato (♩ = 100)

Con espressione

Lancelot:

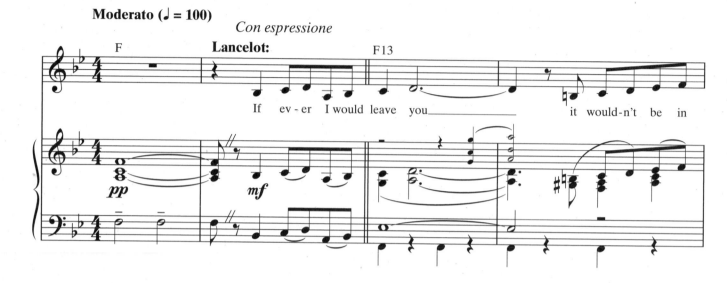

If ev-er I would leave you_____ it would-n't be in

sum-mer;_____ see-ing you in sum-mer, I nev-er would

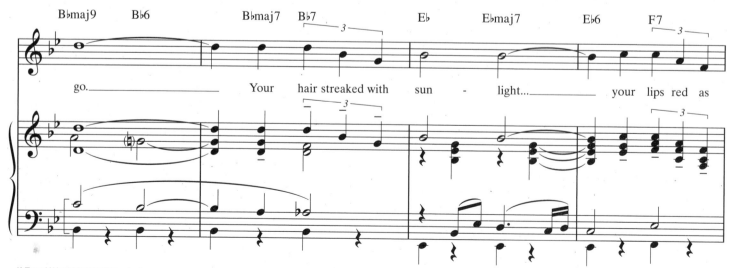

go._____ Your hair streaked with sun - light..... your lips red as

I'M BEGINNING TO SEE THE LIGHT

Words and Music by
DON GEORGE, JOHNNY HODGES,
DUKE ELLINGTON and HARRY JAMES

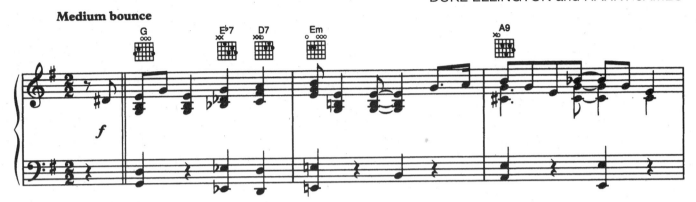

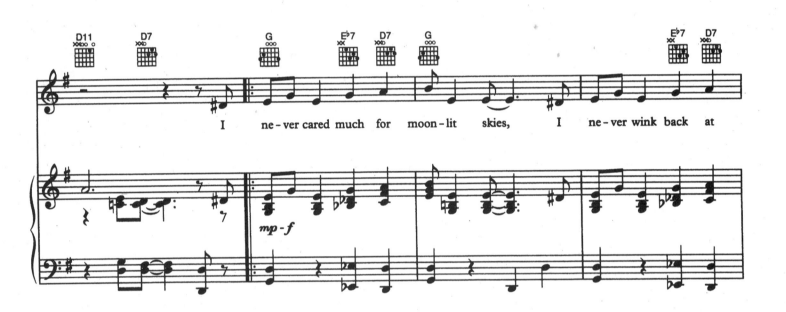

I ne-ver cared much for moon-lit skies, I ne-ver wink back at

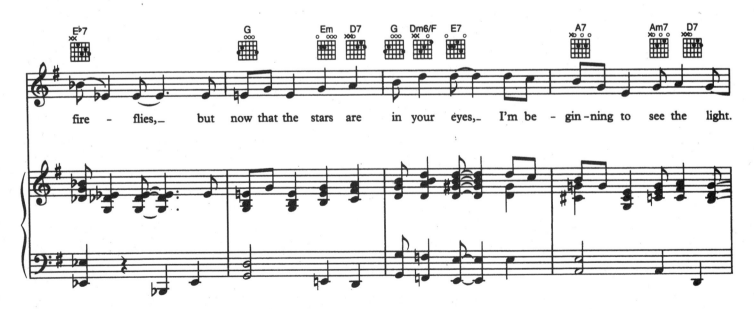

fire - flies,— but now that the stars are in your eyes,— I'm be - gin-ning to see the light.

I'm Beginning to See the Light - 3 - 1

136

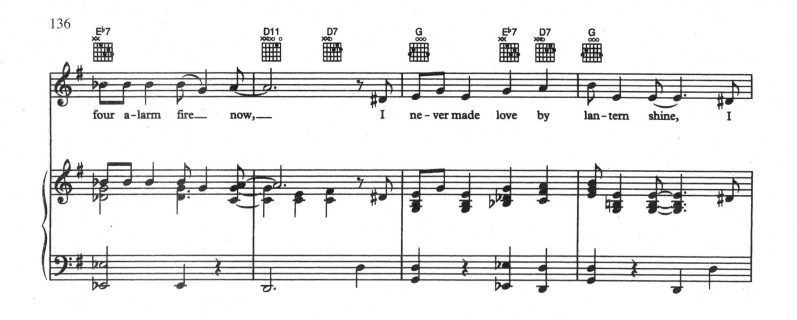

four a-larm fire___ now,___ I ne-ver made love by lan-tern shine, I

ne-ver saw rain-bows in my wine, but now that your lips are burn-ing mine, I'm be-

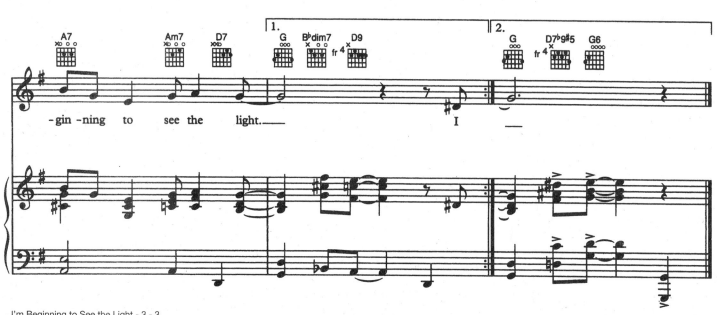

-gin-ning to see the light.___ I ___

I'm Beginning to See the Light - 3 - 3

IT HAD TO BE YOU

Words by
GUS KAHN

Music by
ISHAM JONES

It had to be you,_____ it had to be you._

I wan-dered a-round___ and fi-nal-ly found_

the some-bod-y who_____ could make me be true,_

It Had to Be You - 3 - 1

It Had to Be You - 3 - 3

IT'S MAGIC

Words by
SAMMY CAHN

Music by
JULE STYNE

It's Magic - 4 - 1

142

It's Magic - 4 - 3

I'VE GOT YOU UNDER MY SKIN

Words and Music by
COLE PORTER

IT'S ALL RIGHT WITH ME

Words and Music by
COLE PORTER

It's All Right With Me - 5 - 1

JUST ONE OF THOSE THINGS

Words and Music by
COLE PORTER

Medium swing ♩ = 138

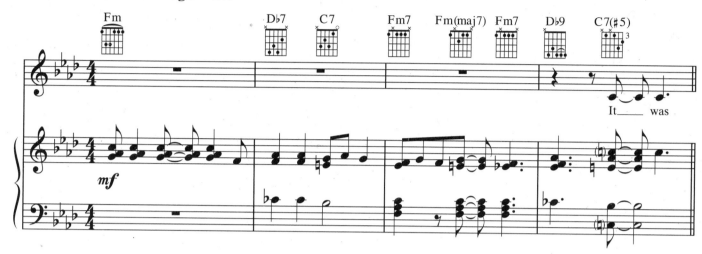

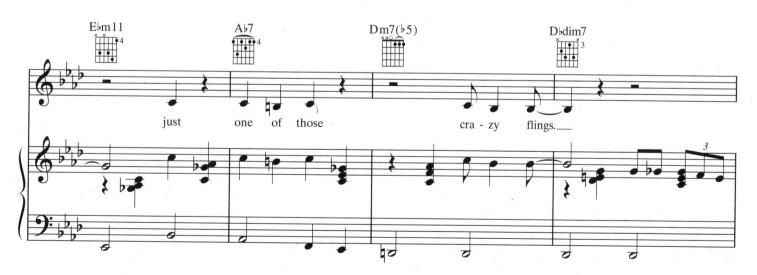

Just One of Those Things - 5 - 1

LA VIE EN ROSE
(Take Me to Your Heart Again)

Original French Lyrics by EDITH PIAF
English Lyrics by MACK DAVID

Music by
LUIS GUGLIELMI

And when you speak, an - gels sing from a - bove. Ev - 'ry day words seem to
C'est luì pour moi, moi pour luì, dans la vie. Il me l'a dit, l'a ju -

turn in - to love songs. Give your heart and soul to me, and life will al - ways
ré pour la vi - e. Et dès que je l'a - per - çois a - lors je sens en

be la vie en rose. rose.
moi mon cúur qui bat. bat.

THE LADY IS A TRAMP

Words by
LORENZ HART

Music by
RICHARD RODGERS

The Lady Is a Tramp - 5 - 1

The Lady Is a Tramp - 5 - 5

LAURA

Lyrics by
JOHNNY MERCER

Music by
DAVID RAKSIN

Lyrics: You know the feel-ing of some-thing half re-mem-bered, of

Laura - 5 - 1

Moderato

Chorus:

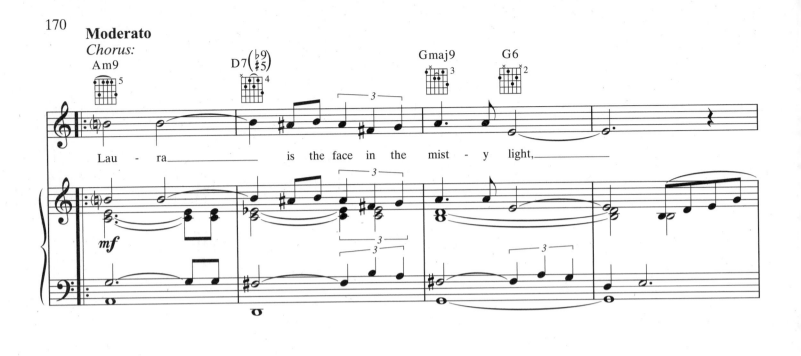

Lau - ra is the face in the mist - y light,

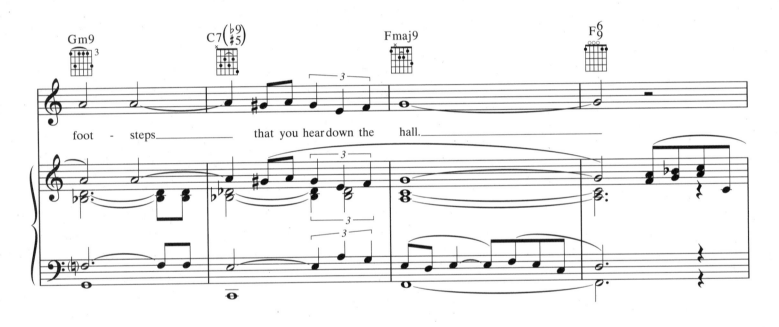

foot - steps that you hear down the hall.

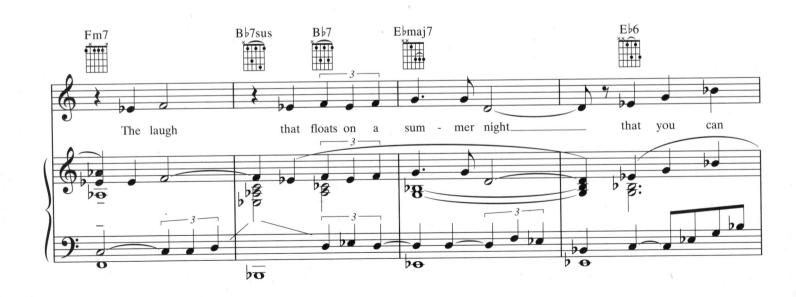

The laugh that floats on a sum - mer night that you can

LONG AGO (AND FAR AWAY)

Lyrics by
IRA GERSHWIN

Music by
JEROME KERN

Long Ago (and Far Away) - 3 - 1

Refrain: (cantabile)

LOOK TO THE RAINBOW

Words by
E.Y. HARBURG

Music by
BURTON LANE

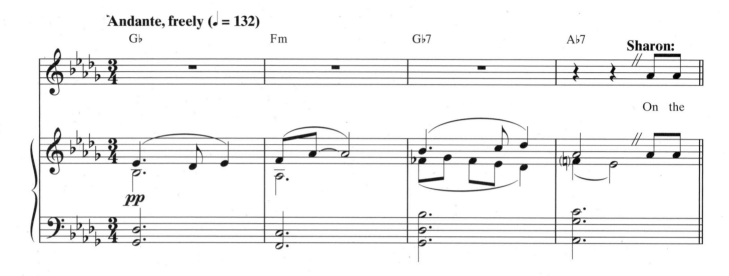

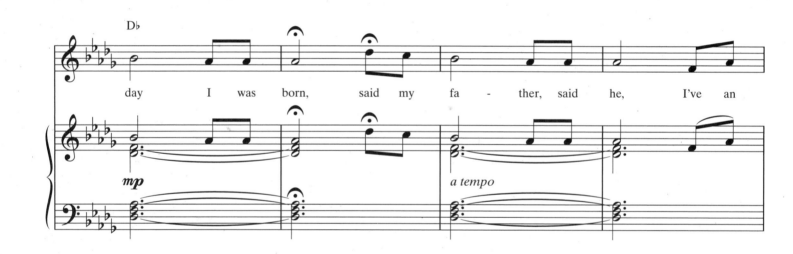

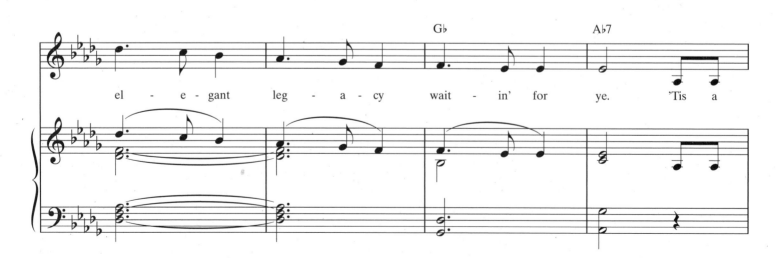

rhyme for your lip___ and a song for your heart,___ to

sing it when - ev - er the world falls a - part.

A tempo, in 3

Look, look, look to the rain - bow.

Fol - low it o - ver the hill___ and stream.

Look to the Rainbow - 5 - 2

searched all the earth,__ and I scanned all the skies,__ but I

found it at last in my own true love's eyes.

Look, look, look to the rain - bow.

Fol - low it o - ver the hill____ and stream.

Look to the Rainbow - 5 - 4

Look, look, look to the rain - bow.

Fol - low the fel - low who fol - lows a dream.

(Woody:) Fol - low the fel - low, fol - low the fel - low.

Sharon: Fol - low the fel - low who fol - lows a dream.

LOVE AND MARRIAGE

Lyric by
SAMMY CAHN

Music by
JAMES VAN HEUSEN

Love and mar - riage, love and mar - riage,

go to - geth - er like a horse and car - riage.
it's an in - sti - tute you can't dis - par - age.

This I tell ya broth - er, ya can't have one with - out the
Ask the lo - cal gen - try and they will. say it's el - e -

Love and Marriage - 3 - 1

Love and Marriage - 3 - 3

LOVE IS HERE TO STAY

Music and Lyrics by
GEORGE GERSHWIN
and IRA GERSHWIN

Con anima

Verse:

The more I read the pa-pers, the less I com-pre-hend the world and all its ca-pers and how it all will

Love Is Here to Stay - 4 - 4

MAKE SOMEONE HAPPY

Lyrics by
BETTY COMDEN
and **ADOLPH GREEN**

Music by
JULE STYNE

Make_____ some-one hap - py; make just one_____ some-one hap - py.

Make just one_____ heart the heart you sing to.

Make Someone Happy - 3 - 1

MISTY

Words by
JOHNNY BURKE

Music by
ERROLL GARNER

THE MORE I SEE YOU

Lyrics by
MACK GORDON

Music by
HARRY WARREN

The More I See You - 4 - 1

more lost with-out you_____ and so it goes._____

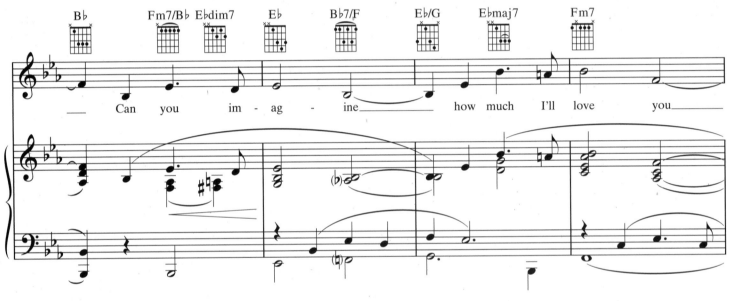

____ Can you im-ag - ine_____ how much I'll love you_____

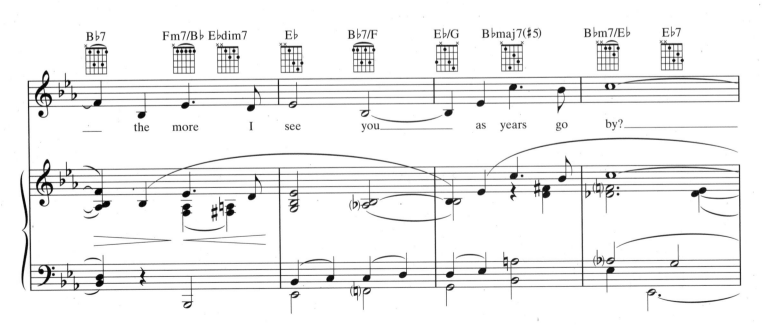

____ the more I see you_____ as years go by?_____

MY FUNNY VALENTINE

Words by
LORENZ HART

Music by
RICHARD RODGERS

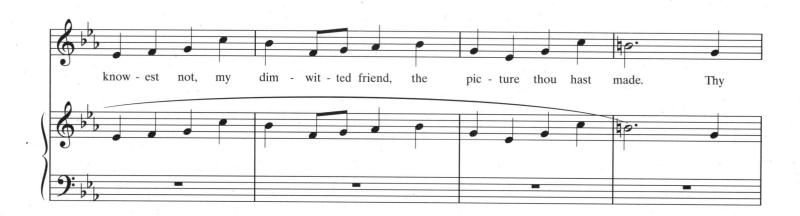

Lyrics under the staves:

va - cant brow and thy tou - sled hair con - ceal thy good in - tent. Thou

no - ble, up - right, truth - ful, sin - cere, and slight - ly dop - ey gent. You're

Slowly, in tempo
Refrain:

my fun - ny val - en - tine, sweet com - ic val - en - tine,

you make me smile with my heart.

NEAR YOU

Words by
KERMIT GOELL

Music by
FRANCIS CRAIG

Some folks like the coun-try, fish-ing in a stream.

Oth-ers like the moun-tains; that's where they can dream.

Near You - 4 - 1

MY SHIP

Lyrics by
IRA GERSHWIN

Music by
KURT WEILL

Andantino cantabile

Refrain:

ship has sails that are made of silk, the decks are trimmed with gold, and of

jam and spice, there's a par-a-dise in the hold._____ My

My Ship - 3 - 1

NIGHT AND DAY

Words and Music by
COLE PORTER

Night and Day - 5 - 1

Night and Day - 5 - 5

ON THE ATCHISON, TOPEKA AND THE SANTA FE

Lyric by
JOHNNY MERCER

Music by
HARRY WARREN

lots o' them been trav-el-in' for quite a spell,___ all the way from Phil-a -

del-phi-ay,___ on the Atch-i-son, To-pe-ka, and the San-ta Fe.___

Do yuh San-ta Fe.___

ON THE STREET WHERE YOU LIVE

Words by
ALAN JAY LERNER

Music by
FREDERICK LOEWE

On the Street Where You Live - 4 - 1

OVER THE RAINBOW

Lyrics by
E.Y. HARBURG

Music by
HAROLD ARLEN

Over the Rainbow - 4 - 1

THE PARTY'S OVER

Lyrics by
BETTY COMDEN and ADOLPH GREEN

Music by
JULE STYNE

I'm in love with a man, but the girl that he loves is-n't me. I'll nev-er see him a-gain, and that's how it has to be. The par-ty's

PEOPLE

Words by
BOB MERRILL

Music by
JULE STYNE

SAVE THE LAST DANCE FOR ME

Words by
DOC POMUS

Music by
MORT SHUMAN

RED ROSES FOR A BLUE LADY

Words and Music by
ROY BENNET and SID TEPPER

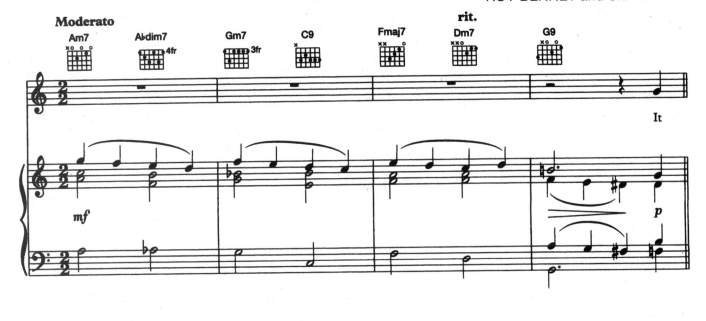

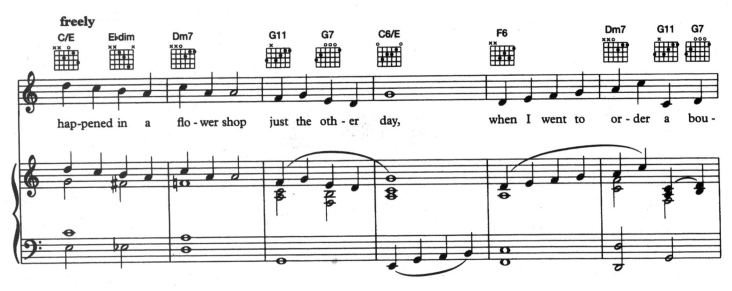

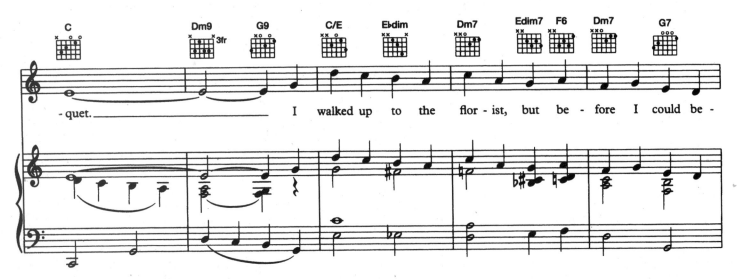

Red Roses for a Blue Lady - 3 - 1

SUMMERTIME

Music and Lyrics by
GEORGE GERSHWIN, IRA GERSHWIN
and DuBOSE and DOROTHY HEYWARD

Summertime - 3 - 1

SINGIN' IN THE RAIN

Lyric by
ARTHUR FREED

Music by
NACIO HERB BROWN

To Coda ⊕

lane with a hap - py re - frain, and sing - in',___ just sing - in' in___ the

G6   E♭7

rain._____

{ Why   am I   smil - in',   and
{ Why   do they call   me   the

G6   E♭7

why do I sing?____   Why   does De - cem - ber   seem
boy with the smile?____   When   did   I   find   out   that

G6   D7

sun - ny   as   spring?____   Why do   I   get   up   each
life is worth - while?____   Why do   I   treat all   my

Singin' in the Rain - 4 - 3

SOMEBODY LOVES ME

Lyrics by
B.G. DeSYLVA and
BALLARD MACDONALD

Music by
GEORGE GERSHWIN

Allegro moderato

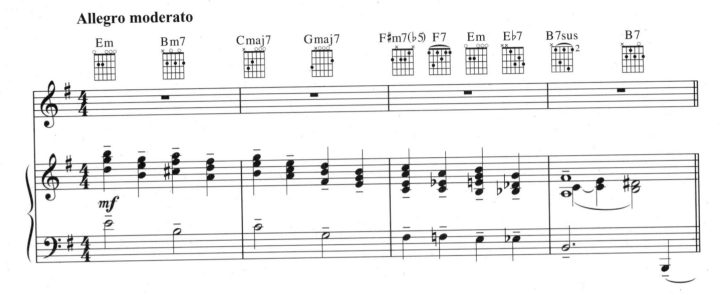

Verse:

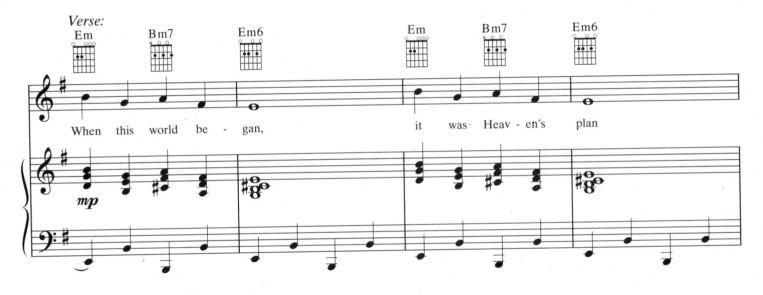

When this world be - gan, it was Heav - en's plan

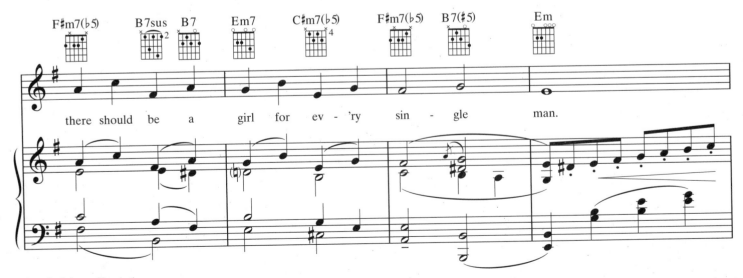

there should be a girl for ev - 'ry sin - gle man.

Somebody Loves Me - 4 - 1

Somebody Loves Me - 4 - 2

248

SOMEONE TO WATCH OVER ME

Music and Lyrics by
GEORGE GERSHWIN
and IRA GERSHWIN

Someone to Watch Over Me - 4 - 1

STAR DUST

Words by
MITCHELL PARISH

Music by
HOAGY CARMICHAEL

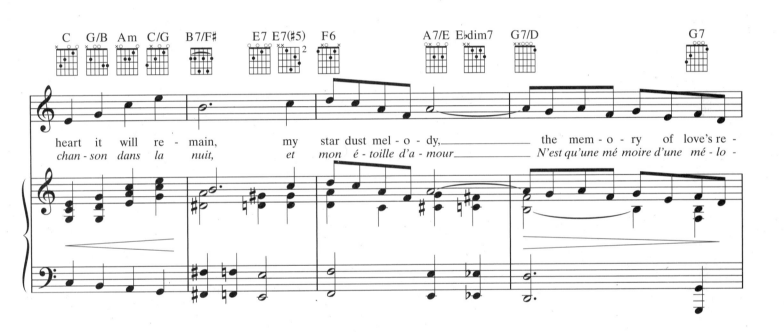

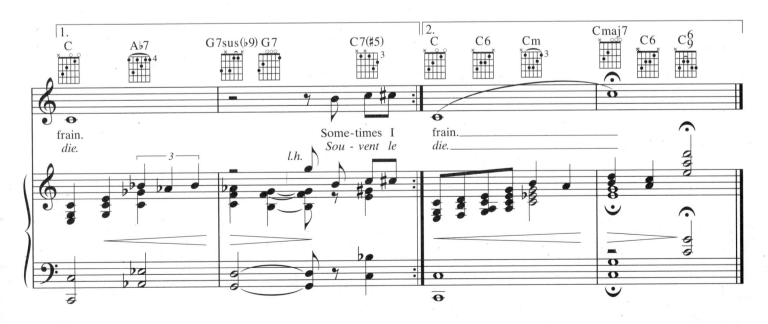

Star Dust - 4 - 4

THE SHADOW OF YOUR SMILE

Lyrics by
PAUL FRANCIS WEBSTER

Music by
JOHNNY MANDEL

Moderately in 2

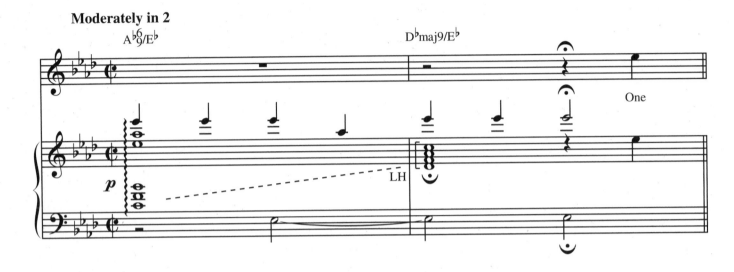

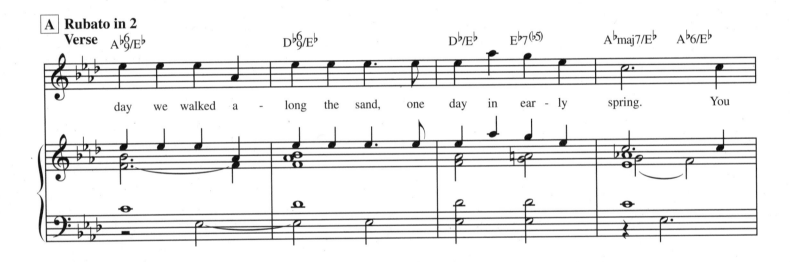

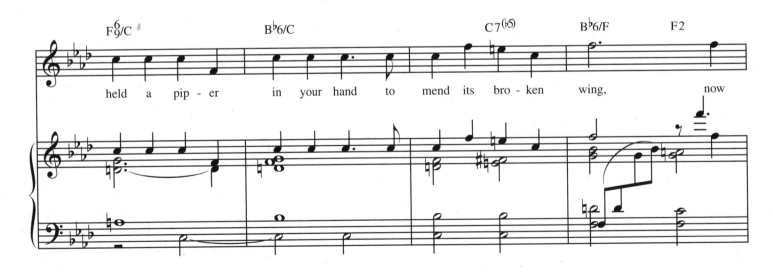

TAKING A CHANCE ON LOVE

Words by
JOHN LATOUCHE
and TED FETTER

Music by
VERNON DUKE

THEY CAN'T TAKE THAT AWAY FROM ME

Music and Lyrics by
GEORGE GERSHWIN
and IRA GERSHWIN

They Can't Take That Away From Me - 4 - 1

THE TROLLEY SONG

Words and Music by
HUGH MARTIN and RALPH BLANE

Chorus: **Brightly**

1. "Clang, clang, clang," went the trol - ley._____ "Ding, ding,
2. "Chug, chug, chug," went the mot - or._____ "Bump, bump,

ding," went the bell._____ "Zing, zing, zing," went my
bump," went the brake._____ "Thump, thump, thump" went my

heart - strings,_____ for the mo - ment I saw {him, her,} I fell.
heart - strings._____ When {he she} smiled, I could feel the car shake.

The Trolley Song - 6 - 6

THREE COINS IN THE FOUNTAIN

Words by
SAMMY CAHN

Music by
JULE STYNE

Three Coins in the Fountain - 3 - 1

TRUE LOVE

Words and Music by
COLE PORTER

True Love - 3 - 1

Refrain:

WHAT A WONDERFUL WORLD

Words and Music by
GEORGE DAVID WEISS and BOB THIELE

What a Wonderful World - 4 - 1

TRY TO REMEMBER

Lyrics by
TOM JONES

Music by
HARVEY SCHMIDT

Slowly, with tenderness (in one)

(with pedal)

Try to re-mem-ber the kind of Sep-tem-ber when
Try to re-mem-ber when life was so ten-der that

life was slow and oh, so mel-low.____
no one wept ex-cept the wil-low.____

Try to Remember - 3 - 1

WHEN I FALL IN LOVE

Words by
EDWARD HEYMAN

Music by
VICTOR YOUNG

When I Fall in Love - 3 - 1

WHERE OR WHEN

Words by
LORENZ HART

Music by
RICHARD RODGERS

YOU STEPPED OUT OF A DREAM

Lyrics by
GUS KAHN

Music by
NACIO HERB BROWN

Freely

Verse:

I've had a mil-lion dreams that nev-er came true

un-til the luck-y day I dis-cov-ered you.

Moderately

Refrain:

You_____ stepped out of a dream,_____ you are too
won - der - ful_____ to be what you seem!_____ Could there be
eyes like yours,_____ could there be lips like yours,_____ could there be

YOU'D BE SO NICE TO COME HOME TO

Words and Music by
COLE PORTER

Verse 2:
She: I should be excited,
But, Lothario, why not own up
That you always chase
After every new face in town?
I would be delighted
If we two could, some day, be sewn up.
For if you behaved like a grown-up
And could only slow down.
(Repeat Refrain)

YOU'LL NEVER KNOW

Lyrics by
MACK GORDON

Music by
HARRY WARREN

Dar-ling, I'm so blue with-

out you.___ I think a-bout you___ the live-long day.

When you ask me if I'm lone-ly,___ then I have on-ly this to say:

You'll Never Know - 4 - 1

Refrain:

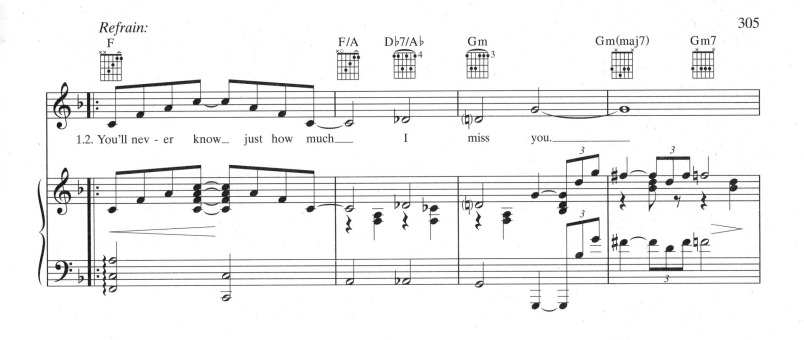

1.2. You'll nev - er know just how much I miss you.

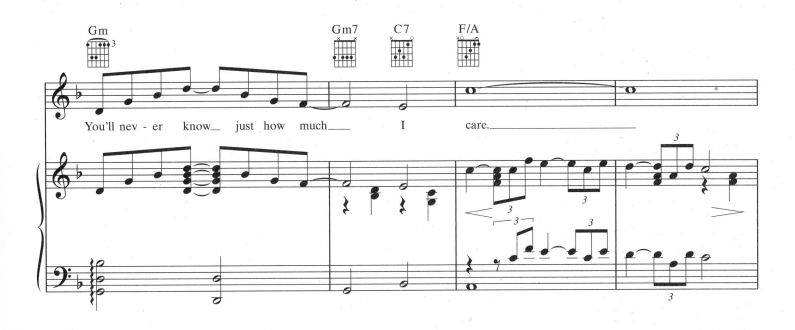

You'll nev - er know just how much I care.

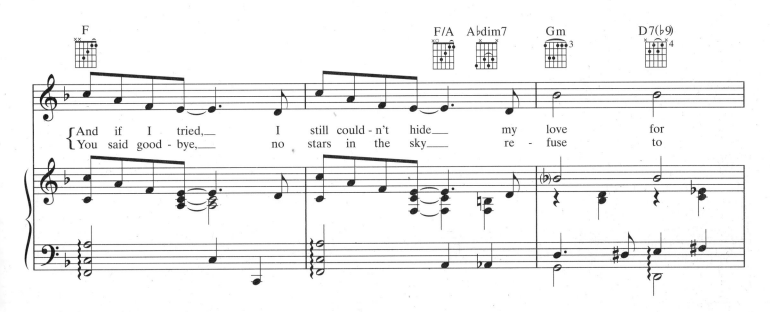

And if I tried, I still could - n't hide my love for
You said good - bye, no stars in the sky re - fuse to

If there is some oth-er way to prove that I love you, I swear, I don't know how. You'll nev-er know if you don't know now.

1. know now.

2. now.

Comsewogue Public Library
170 Terryville Road
Port Jefferson Station, NY 11776

Alfred